THE
5-MINUTE
5-Ingredient
LUNCHBOX

THE
5-MINUTE
5-Ingredient
LUNCHBOX

HAPPY, HEALTHY & SPEEDY
MEALS TO MAKE
IN MINUTES

ALEXANDER HART

Smith Street Books

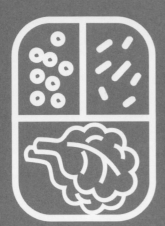

CONTENTS

INTRODUCTION

~~~~~

If you've opened this book, you're probably someone who is pretty short on time. Sprinting out the front door every morning, late for the train. Busy herding sleepy-eyed kids into the car. Or just overly fond of the snooze button. All these are valid reasons to skip the step of preparing your own lunch in the morning. But it's time to shake things up.

At first it might seem hard to break the cycle of buying lunch every day. And maybe you work next to the best deli in the country. Sure. But the cost of those meals adds up. You'll be amazed by the money you can save by preparing your own lunches. Plus, there's the added bonus of knowing exactly what goes into each and every bite. And all you need is 5 minutes and 5 ingredients.

The chapters that follow separate ideas for simple and speedy lunches into five handy categories: Wraps, Beans & Legumes, Grains & Seeds, Noodles & Zoodles and Bento Boxes. At the back of this book you'll also find the recipes for all the dressings used throughout – but feel free to use store-bought. If that little timesaver means you actually commit to preparing your own lunch every day, do so with pride.

Each recipe in this book uses 5 ingredients. Dressing counts as one. But – quick disclaimer – in the Wrap chapter, the wrap isn't counted in our 5-ingredient tally. It's merely a tasty vessel for your lunch, after all.

Spending one day a week prepping all your lunches is one way to guarantee you've got something to grab as you're leaving for work. But even if you are preparing some of these recipes in bulk, try to make a few different recipes for the coming week. Besides providing you with variety – the spice of life – this will make sure that you're sneaking into your diet the broadest possible spectrum of nutrients.

One more thing. If you're someone whose job leaves you feeling constantly stressed, try not to eat these tasty lunchboxes sitting at your desk. Or behind a counter. Or in a windowless break room. The best antidote to stress in our work lives are moments of calm. So, weather permitting, grab your packed 5-Minute, 5-Ingredient Lunchbox and head outside for 20 minutes. Leave your phone behind for extra points – all you really need is a fork.

SALAD INGREDIENTS

Here are a few notes on some of the ingredients used in this book, along with tips and tricks to help cut down your prep time even further.

BEANS & LENTILS

Although the recipes in this book call for tinned beans and lentils – as they're a speedy option for adding to salads and wraps – you can, of course, soak and cook your own beans and lentils ahead of time and store them in the fridge. One of the major advantages to this is that you avoid the salt and sugar of the brine that tinned varieties are stored in.

BEETROOT

Cooked beetroot (beets) are available from the supermarket, usually found in vacuum-sealed packets, tins or jars. Mix it up and use golden or striped beetroot when they're in season.

COOKED CHICKEN

Shredded cooked chicken is available in most supermarket delis. Alternatively, buy or cook a whole roast chicken, chop or shred the meat yourself and store in an airtight container in the fridge for up to 4 days. Another healthy option (if you have time) is to poach some chicken breasts for use throughout the week.

CORN

Some of the recipes call for tinned sweet corn; however, if you have more time, chargrill a fresh corn cob instead. Slice off the kernels and add to your lunchbox with the remaining salad ingredients. Alternatively, you can cook the corn ahead of time and keep the kernels in an airtight container in the fridge for up to 3 days.

DRESSINGS

For most of the recipes in this book, the dressing is kept separately so you can dress your salad just before you eat it. You can save yourself some more time in the morning by mixing your dressing the night before and keeping the container in the fridge – you could even prep a whole week's worth in advance.

GRAINS & NOODLES

Bulgur
The recipes in this book allow bulgur to soak and 'cook' in the time between preparing your salad in the morning and eating it at lunchtime. If you have

time to prepare it the night before (and you'd rather not take an extra jar with you), make the bulgur according to the packet instructions and store in an airtight container in the fridge for up to 4 days.

Instant (ramen) noodles

Check the packet instructions, but these should cook in boiling water in 2–3 minutes. Rinse under cold water and drain.

Quinoa & brown rice

These days there are various 'quick' and 'instant' quinoa and brown rice products available that are ready in 2–3 minutes. Cook according to the packet instructions and allow to cool. Alternatively, if you have time to prep regular quinoa or brown rice ahead of time, cook a large batch according to the packet instructions, then cool and store in an airtight container in the fridge for up to 4 days. Even easier, make enough for leftovers when cooking quinoa or brown rice for dinner, then simply toss with the remaining salad ingredients in the morning. If you can, try using a combination of black, red and white varieties of quinoa to mix things up a little.

Soba noodles

Cook according to the packet instructions. Rinse well under cold water and drain.

Vermicelli noodles

To prepare vermicelli noodles, place in a bowl, cover with boiling water and allow to sit for 3–4 minutes, giving them a bit of a stir occasionally to loosen them. Rinse under cold water and drain.

HARD-BOILED EGGS

Make a batch ahead of time and keep in the fridge for up to 1 week. To cook them, place your eggs in a saucepan and cover with cold water. Bring to the boil over medium–high heat, then cover, remove from the heat and set aside for 8–11 minutes (depending on how hard-boiled you like them). Drain, cool in iced water and peel just before adding to your salad.

HERBS

To save time, chop all of your fresh herbs together.

MINCED GARLIC AND GINGER

Available in jars – or tubes (usually sold as 'paste') – from the supermarket, these really are a time-saving wonder. Alternatively, you can make your own: blitz a large quantity of garlic or fresh ginger in your food processor with a little water, salt and a drop of olive oil. It will keep well in an airtight container in the fridge for up to 2 weeks, or press flat in a zip-lock bag and store in the freezer for up to 2 months.

PRE-CUT VEGETABLES

Supermarkets now carry a large range of packaged pre-cut vegetables that keep really well in your fridge, which is what we recommend using to keep your prep time to around 5 minutes. Look out for broccoli or cauliflower 'rice'; shredded carrot, cabbage and lettuce; spiralised zucchini / courgette (zoodles) and beetroot (beets); and other convenient combination products, such as coleslaw and mixed salad leaves.

TOASTED NUTS & SEEDS

Toast nuts and seeds ahead of time, leave to cool completely, then store them in an airtight container in your pantry for up to 1 month.

WRAPS

There are many different types of wraps available – some wheat-based, some gluten-free, some flavoured and coloured with natural ingredients including beetroot (beet), spinach and tomato. Feel free to use whatever you like for those wrap recipes.

NOTES ON QUANTITIES

We find you rarely need exact quantities when putting together a salad, so we've used 'handfuls of' in many cases, making ingredients quick to throw in. Feel free to adjust the quantities to make use of what you might already have in your fridge.

All tablespoons are 15 ml / 3 teaspoons.

WRAPS

SMOKED CHICKEN RANCH WRAP

Smoked chicken breast is a great choice if you want to add some delicious smoky flavour to your salad without fussing around with multiple ingredients. You can buy it from butchers, delis and supermarkets.

1 wrap

handful of roughly torn cos (romaine) lettuce
100 g (3½ oz) smoked chicken breast, diced
1 small celery stalk, diced
¼ avocado, sliced
Ranch mayonnaise, store-bought or see recipe on page 126

1 Top the wrap with all the ingredients.

2 Roll up and secure the wrap.

TURKEY, GRUYÈRE & KALE WRAP

The perfect lunchtime treat – a deliciously moreish wrap
with turkey, apple, kale, cheese and a creamy dressing.

1 wrap

handful of finely shredded kale
¼ granny smith apple, julienned
4 slices honey-roasted turkey breast
30 g (1 oz) grated gruyère
Honey mustard mayonnaise, store-bought or see recipe on page 125

1 Top the wrap with all the ingredients.

2 Roll up and secure the wrap.

SMOKED SALMON WRAP

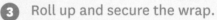

This wrap is a play on the classic smoked salmon bagel. Herbed cream cheese will keep in your fridge for at least a week – so you can whip it up on the weekend for the week of lunches ahead.

1 wrap

Herbed cream cheese, store-bought or see recipe on page 125

handful of mixed baby greens

½ short cucumber, sliced into thin ribbons

70 g (2½ oz) smoked salmon

¼ red onion, thinly sliced

1 Spread the herbed cream cheese over the wrap.

2 Top the wrap with the remaining ingredients.

3 Roll up and secure the wrap.

FALAFEL WRAP

Falafel wraps are loved across much of the Middle East – and increasingly around the world. They make a filling vegetarian lunch. Falafel balls can be bought from the supermarket or from falafel shops, and are usually made from chickpeas or broad (fava) beans – or a mixture of both.

1 wrap

3–4 falafel balls, roughly torn

handful of torn cos (romaine) lettuce

½ tomato, diced

some Turkish pickled turnips, chopped

Tahini yoghurt sauce, store-bought or see recipe on page 127

1 Top the wrap with all the ingredients.

2 Roll up and secure the wrap.

ULTIMATE AVOCADO GREEN GODDESS WRAP

Take a trip back to 1970s California, where the green goddess dressing was ubiquitous. A nutritious, delicious wrap in every bite.

1 spinach wrap

3 tablespoons green hummus or regular hummus

handful of baby spinach leaves

handful of alfalfa sprouts

½ avocado, sliced

Green goddess dressing, store-bought or see recipe on page 124

1. Spread the hummus over the wrap.

2. Top the wrap with the remaining ingredients.

3. Roll up and secure the wrap.

SUBMARINE WRAP

~~~

This is a wrap version of a classic 'sub' roll that uses a selection of deli meats, cheese, tomato and lettuce. It packs all the flavour – but without the heaviness of so much bread!

◇◇◇◇◇◇◇◇◇◇

1 wrap

3 slices each of mortadella, salami and ham

2 slices of provolone cheese

1 roma (plum) tomato, sliced

handful of shredded cos (romaine) lettuce

Italian vinaigrette, store-bought or see recipe on page 125

1. Top the wrap with all the ingredients.
2. Roll up and secure the wrap.

CAPRESE WRAP

The caprese salad can be found on menus all across Italy – with the colours in the dish mimicking the green, white and red of the Italian flag. Here, we tie up all these wonderful flavours in a handy wrap!

◇◇◇◇◇◇◇◇◇◇

1 sun-dried tomato wrap

handful of rocket (arugula)

small handful of heirloom cherry tomatoes, sliced

½ fresh mozzarella ball, sliced

¼ red onion, thinly sliced

Pesto mayo dressing, store-bought or see recipe on page 126

1 Top the wrap with all the ingredients.

2 Roll up and secure the wrap.

CHICKEN TANDOORI WRAP

A delicious, tangy wrap with bursts of flavour from the fresh mango and yoghurt sauce. If you prefer, this would also make a great salad – simply replace the wrap with rice, mix it all together and stir the sauce through just before serving.

◇◇◇◇◇◇◇◇◇◇◇

1 wrap

120 g (4½ oz) shredded cooked chicken

Tandoori yoghurt sauce, store-bought or see recipe on page 127

¼ small red onion, thinly sliced

¼ short cucumber, thinly sliced

¼ mango, sliced

1 Toss the chicken in the tandoori yoghurt sauce.

2 Top the wrap with all the ingredients.

3 Roll up and secure the wrap.

MEXICAN PRAWN
CAESAR WRAP

This recipe calls for cotija cheese – a hard, salty, cow's milk cheese originating in the town of Cotija, Mexico. If available, it's a great, authentic addition to this wrap. Otherwise, go for a crumbly feta cheese instead.

1 wrap

handful of torn cos (romaine) lettuce
½ avocado, sliced
5–6 large cooked peeled prawns (shrimp)
2 tablespoons crumbled Mexican cotija cheese, or feta
Coriander caesar dressing, store-bought or see recipe on page 124

1 Top the wrap with all the ingredients.

2 Roll up and secure the wrap.

TAHINI CHICKPEA
SALAD WRAP

With its brilliant combination of ingredients, this spinach wrap is a vegan equivalent of tuna salad. It has much of the flavour and texture of a tuna wrap, to satisfy any meat-eater.

1 spinach wrap

80 g (2¾ oz) drained tinned chickpeas

½ celery stalk, finely diced

¼ red onion, finely diced

handful of mixed salad greens

Tahini sauce, store-bought or see recipe on page 127

1. Roughly mash the chickpeas in a bowl.

2. Mix in the celery and onion.

3. Top the wrap with all the ingredients.

4. Roll up and secure the wrap.

FESTIVE TURKEY WRAP

This wrap can be enjoyed any time of the year – but in holiday season, you can also replace the sliced turkey breast with left-over roast turkey.

1 wrap

3 tablespoons cream cheese
1 tablespoon cranberry relish
handful of rocket (arugula) leaves
80 g (2¾ oz) sliced smoked turkey breast
1 tablespoon chopped honey-spiced pecans

1 Spread the cream cheese over the wrap.

2 Top the wrap with the remaining ingredients.

3 Roll up and secure the wrap.

CRUNCHY RAINBOW WRAP

Here's a wrap bursting with colour, flavour and vitality! To save the time of spiralising the vegetables yourself, many supermarkets sell pre-spiralised and pre-mixed vegetables.

1 sun-dried tomato wrap

2 large handfuls of spiralised vegetables, such as carrot, beetroot (beet) and zucchini (courgette)

small handful of parsley leaves

½ avocado, sliced

1 teaspoon toasted sesame seeds

Lemony tahini dressing, store-bought or see recipe on page 125

1. Top the wrap with all the ingredients.
2. Roll up and secure the wrap.

SMOKED TROUT WRAP

Smoked trout combines beautifully with the other ingredients in this wrap – but, if you prefer, you could swap it out with flaked, tinned tuna.

1 spinach wrap

---

75 g (2½ oz) smoked trout, flaked

1 hard-boiled egg, peeled and quartered

handful of watercress sprigs

½ avocado, sliced

Horseradish mayonnaise, store-bought or see recipe on page 125

1 Top the wrap with all the ingredients.

2 Roll up and secure the wrap.

BEANS
+
LEGUMES

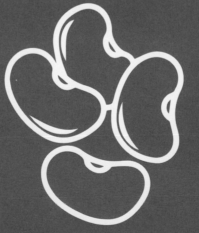

MIDDLE EASTERN BEAN SALAD

Here you'll find a healthy mixture of beans and salad greens, with the sweetness of dried cranberries – also sold as 'craisins'. Feel free to replace the spinach leaves with whatever pre-mixed salad greens are available.

150 g (5½ oz) drained tinned four-bean mix

½ short cucumber, sliced

2 handfuls of baby spinach leaves

2 tablespoon dried cranberries

Pomegranate dressing, store-bought or see recipe on page 126

1 Toss the salad ingredients together with salt and pepper to taste, then tip into your lunchbox.

2 Pour the dressing over the salad just before serving and toss well.

SICILIAN OLIVE, TUNA & CANNELLINI BEAN SALAD

Drawing inspiration from Italy, this salad is a breeze to put together. If you prefer yours without spice, go for tinned tuna in olive oil instead of one infused with chilli. Sicilian green olives have a buttery, meaty texture and a mild taste. They're widely available in most supermarkets.

95 g (3¼ oz) tin tuna in chilli oil, drained

100 g (3½ oz) drained tinned cannellini beans

small handful of pitted Sicilian green olives

2 handfuls of mixed salad greens

Parsley & caper dressing, store-bought or see recipe on page 125

1 Toss the salad ingredients together with salt and pepper to taste, then tip into your lunchbox.

2 Pour the dressing over the salad just before serving and toss well.

CHORIZO, ROASTED RED CAPSICUM & BORLOTTI BEAN SALAD

Chorizo is the star of this deliciously tasty and hearty Spanish-style salad. There are many varieties of chorizo, but they fall under two broad styles – fresh and dry. Fresh chorizo, as the name suggests, needs to be cooked before it is consumed. Dry, or smoked chorizo, such as the one called for here, can be eaten without any cooking or preparation.

150 g (5½ oz) drained tinned borlotti (cranberry) beans

80 g (2¾ oz) smoked chorizo, sliced

2 marinated roasted red capsicums (bell peppers), sliced

2 handfuls of rocket (arugula)

Parsley & paprika dressing, store-bought or see recipe on page 125

1. Toss the salad ingredients together with salt and pepper to taste, then tip into your lunchbox.

2. Pour the dressing over the salad just before serving and toss well.

SPICY BLACK BEAN & QUINOA SALAD

~~~~~~~~

Black beans, avocado, tomato and jalapeños evoke the flavours of Mexico, combined with the taste and texture of quinoa – a grain-like seed with Bolivian and Peruvian origins. Quinoa comes in red, white and black varieties – sometimes mixed together and sold as tricolour quinoa – but any type will work here.

◇◇◇◇◇◇◇◇◇◇◇

100 g (3½ oz) drained tinned black beans

150 g (5½ oz/1 cup) cooked and cooled quinoa

handful of cherry tomatoes, halved

½ avocado, diced

Spicy jalapeño dressing, store-bought or see recipe on page 127

1 Toss the salad ingredients together with salt and pepper to taste, then tip into your lunchbox.

2 Pour the dressing over the salad just before serving and toss well.

LENTIL, RICOTTA & BEETROOT SALAD

A treat for the eyes, this beautiful, colourful salad hums with delicious, fresh flavours. Yellow or golden beetroot isn't always easy to find – but can be simply replaced with regular red beetroot.

150 g (5½ oz / ⅔ cup) drained tinned lentils

100 g (3½ oz) raw yellow beetroot (beet), very thinly sliced

50 g (1¾ oz) ricotta, crumbled

handful of radicchio leaves, torn

White balsamic dressing, store-bought or see recipe on page 127

1 Toss the salad ingredients together with salt and pepper to taste, then tip into your lunchbox.

2 Pour the dressing over the salad just before serving and toss well.

CRUNCHY GREENS & LENTIL SALAD

There's nothing like the satisfying crunch of a healthy salad. Here, it's the sugar snap peas that provide that delicious textural bite!

150 g (5½ oz/⅔ cup) drained tinned lentils

100 g (3½ oz) sugar snap peas, blanched

3 broccolini stems, blanched, cut into 5 cm (2 inch) lengths

handful of baby spinach leaves

Sesame & ginger dressing, store-bought or see recipe on page 126

1 Toss the salad ingredients together with salt and pepper to taste, then tip into your lunchbox.

2 Pour the dressing over the salad just before serving and toss well.

CHICKEN, LENTIL & CAPER SALAD

Here's a great use for left-over cooked chicken – which could be left-over roast or poached chicken, or even pre-bought barbecued chicken. To shred the chicken, use two forks or clean hands to pull it apart.

◇◇◇◇◇◇◇◇◇◇◇

150 g (5½ oz cup/⅔ cup) drained tinned lentils

100 g (3½ oz) shredded cooked chicken

large handful of mixed small heirloom tomatoes, halved

handful of baby capers

Preserved lemon & honey dressing, store-bought or see recipe on page 126

1 Toss the salad ingredients together with salt and pepper to taste, then tip into your lunchbox.

2 Pour the dressing over the salad just before serving and toss well.

CHICKPEA, CARROT & DILL SALAD

This vegan-friendly salad is super quick to
put together. To save even more time in the kitchen,
buy pre-shredded carrot from the supermarket
rather than shredding the carrot yourself.

150 g (5½ oz) drained tinned chickpeas

large handful of shredded carrot

large handful of roughly chopped dill

1 celery stalk, thinly sliced

Lemon dressing, store-bought or see recipe on page 125

1 Toss the salad ingredients together with salt and pepper to taste, then tip into your lunchbox.

2 Pour the dressing over the salad just before serving and toss well.

SPICY BLACK-EYED BEAN, CORN & CORIANDER SALAD

Black-eyed beans have an earthy, nutty flavour that combines well with the other ingredients in this salad. If you find the tinned version hard to come by, simply replace them with black beans.

◇◇◇◇◇◇◇◇◇◇◇

150 g (5½ oz) drained tinned black-eyed beans

75 g (2¾ oz) drained tinned sweet corn kernels

¼ red capsicum (bell pepper), finely diced

large handful of coriander (cilantro) leaves

Jalapeño yoghurt dressing, store-bought or see recipe on page 125

1. Toss the salad ingredients together with salt and pepper to taste, then tip into your lunchbox.

2. Pour the dressing over the salad just before serving and toss well.

GRAINS

+

SEEDS

JAPANESE EDAMAME & BROWN RICE SALAD

Edamame beans – or soy beans – are available in the freezer section of some supermarkets and in Asian grocers. They make a great snack on their own, sprinkled with some sea salt.

3 broccolini stems

80 g (2¾ oz/ ½ cup) frozen edamame beans

150 g (5½ oz/1 cup) cooked and cooled brown rice

½ avocado, sliced

Sesame miso dressing, store-bought or see recipe on page 126

1 Blanch the broccolini and edamame beans in boiling salted water for 2 minutes. Drain and refresh in cold water, then slice the broccolini into 5 cm (2 inch) pieces.

2 Toss with the remaining salad ingredients with salt and pepper to taste, then tip into your lunchbox.

3 Pour the dressing over the salad just before serving and toss well.

JAPANESE CHICKEN & RICE SALAD WITH GINGER SOY DRESSING

If you prefer a nuttier flavour – and a little more fibre – in your salad, opt for brown rice here. Micro herbs can be found in most good-quality greengrocers.

150 g (5½ oz/1 cup) cooked and cooled rice

100 g (3½ oz) shredded cooked chicken

50 g (1¾ oz) snow peas (mangetout), sliced

large handful of mixed micro herbs

Ginger soy dressing, store-bought or see recipe on page 124

1 Toss the salad ingredients together with salt and pepper to taste, then tip into your lunchbox.

2 Pour the dressing over the salad just before serving and toss well.

SALMON POKE BOWL
WITH BLACK RICE

Poke – pronounced *po-kay* – bowls first originated in Hawaii, but are now loved around the world. They typically contain raw fish, rice and salad, and make a quick, nutritious lunch.

150 g (5½ oz/1 cup) cooked and cooled black rice

100 g (3½ oz) raw sashimi-grade salmon, diced

½ avocado, diced

75 g (2½ oz/½ cup) podded cooked edamame beans

Sweet chilli soy dressing, store-bought or see recipe on page 127

1 Toss the salad ingredients together with salt and pepper to taste, then tip into your lunchbox.

2 Pour the dressing over the salad just before serving and toss well.

PERSIAN COUSCOUS SALAD

Moreish dried fruits and nutty pistachios combined with couscous and shredded chicken – what a delight! This hearty couscous-based salad is a feast for the senses.

150 g (5½ oz/1 cup) cooked and cooled couscous

100 g (3½ oz) shredded cooked chicken

70 g (2½ oz) diced mixed dried fruits (apricot, cherries, figs)

2 tablespoons chopped pistachios

Lemon & sumac dressing, store-bought or see recipe on page 125

1 Toss the salad ingredients together with salt and pepper to taste, then tip into your lunchbox.

2 Pour the dressing over the salad just before serving and toss well.

RED QUINOA AUTUMN SALAD

Feel free to replace the red kale leaves in this beautiful, flavoursome salad with green kale, or whatever salad greens you have at hand. Kale can be a little tough to chew through, so to tenderise the leaves ahead of time, massage the leaves with a little lemon juice.

◇◇◇◇◇◇◇◇◇◇

150 g (5½ oz/1 cup) cooked and cooled red quinoa

handful of chopped red kale leaves

100 g (3½ oz) smoked chicken breast, sliced

2 tablespoons toasted walnuts, chopped

Sherry vinegar & shallot dressing, store-bought or see recipe on page 126

1 Toss the salad ingredients together with salt and pepper to taste, then tip into your lunchbox.

2 Pour the dressing over the salad just before serving and toss well.

COUSCOUS, TOMATO, CUCUMBER & FETA SALAD

Juicy tomatoes, salty, creamy feta and crisp, crunchy cucumber evoke memories of the Mediterranean in this simple couscous salad. A creamy, tangy dill dressing plays a perfect complement.

150 g (5½ oz/1 cup) cooked and cooled couscous

1 short cucumber, sliced

handful of cherry tomatoes, halved

40 g (1½ oz) feta cheese, crumbled

Creamy dill dressing, store-bought or see recipe on page 124

1 Toss the salad ingredients together with salt and pepper to taste, then tip into your lunchbox.

2 Pour the dressing over the salad just before serving and toss well.

BLACK QUINOA &
ROASTED PUMPKIN SALAD

This recipe calls for left-over pumpkin, but this can easily be replaced with whatever left-over roast vegetables you may have available, including sweet potato, carrot, zucchini (courgette) or potato.

150 g (5½ oz/1 cup) cooked and cooled black quinoa

200 g (7 oz) left-over roasted pumpkin (winter squash), diced

large handful of chopped kale

2 tablespoons honey-spiced almonds or pecans, some chopped

Sherry vinegar & mustard dressing, store-bought or see recipe on page 126

1. Toss the salad ingredients together with salt and pepper to taste, then tip into your lunchbox.

2. Pour the dressing over the salad just before serving and toss well.

BULGUR & ROASTED VEG SALAD

The harissa in the dressing really gives this tasty salad a little spark. Feel free to increase the amount used if you like a little more heat.

150 g (5½ oz/1 cup) cooked and cooled bulgur

200 g (7 oz) leftover roasted baby vegetables

100 g (3½ oz) drained tinned chickpeas

handful of mint leaves

Harissa yoghurt dressing, store-bought or see recipe on page 125

1 Toss the salad ingredients together with salt and pepper to taste, then tip into your lunchbox.

2 Pour the dressing over the salad just before serving and toss well.

CHICKEN, MINT & COUSCOUS SALAD

If you wanted to add a few more ingredients to this 5-ingredient salad, you could always throw in a few different types of herbs. Parsley or basil would be good additions, or you could add coriander (cilantro) instead.

150 g (5½ oz/1 cup) cooked and cooled couscous

100 g (3½ oz) shredded cooked chicken

large handful of roughly torn mint leaves

3 tablespoons currants

Lemon dressing, store-bought or see recipe on page 125

1 Toss the salad ingredients together with salt and pepper to taste, then tip into your lunchbox.

2 Pour the dressing over the salad just before serving and toss well.

NOODLES

+

ZOODLES

HOKKIEN NOODLE & SNOW PEA SALAD

Orange segments in the salad and juice in the dressing
add a zesty citrus note to this fresh noodle salad.
This salad also works well with soba or instant
(ramen) noodles instead of the hokkien noodles.

150 g (5½ oz) cooked thin hokkien
(egg) noodles, rinsed and drained

100 g (3½ oz) snow peas
(mangetout), halved

1 small orange, segmented

¼ avocado, sliced

Almond miso dressing, store-
bought or see recipe on page 124

1 Toss the salad ingredients together
with salt and pepper to taste, then tip
into your lunchbox.

2 Pour the dressing over the salad just
before serving and toss well.

SOBA NOODLE, TOFU & SUGAR SNAP PEA SALAD

In this Japanese-inspired noodle salad, the texture of silken tofu plays against the crunch of the radish and sugar snap peas. The dressing adds sharpness through wasabi, but if you prefer your salad without spice, simply omit it from the dressing.

180 g (6½ oz) cooked, rinsed and drained soba noodles

100 g (3½ oz) sugar snap peas, blanched

50 g (1¾ oz) silken tofu, cubed

2 radishes, thinly sliced

Soy & wasabi dressing, store-bought or see recipe on page 127

1 Toss the salad ingredients together with salt and pepper to taste, then tip into your lunchbox.

2 Pour the dressing over the salad just before serving and toss well.

SPICY RAMEN NOODLE & CHICKEN SALAD

The dressing in this recipe calls for sriracha – a hot, spicy red sauce. If you prefer to avoid spice, omit it or use Tabasco or another sauce instead.

200 g (7 oz) instant (ramen) noodles, cooked, rinsed and drained

50 g (1¾ oz) sugar snap peas, sliced and blanched

100 g (3½ oz) shredded cooked chicken

2 handfuls of baby spinach leaves

Spicy peanut dressing, store-bought or see recipe on page 127

1 Toss the salad ingredients together with salt and pepper to taste, then tip into your lunchbox.

2 Pour the dressing over the salad just before serving and toss well.

GREEN TEA NOODLES WITH SALMON & CRUNCHY GREENS

~~~

Green tea is a popular flavour in Japan, where it's added to sweets, as well as savoury foods, including soba noodles. It pairs beautifully with the raw salmon, green beans and cucumber in this dish.

◇◇◇◇◇◇◇◇◇◇

180 g (6½ oz) cooked, rinsed and drained green tea soba noodles

50 g (1¾ oz) green beans, sliced and blanched

85 g (3 oz) raw sashimi-grade salmon, sliced

½ short cucumber, thinly sliced

Sesame miso dressing, store-bought or see recipe on page 126

1 Toss the salad ingredients together with salt and pepper to taste, then tip into your lunchbox.

2 Pour the dressing over the salad just before serving and toss well.

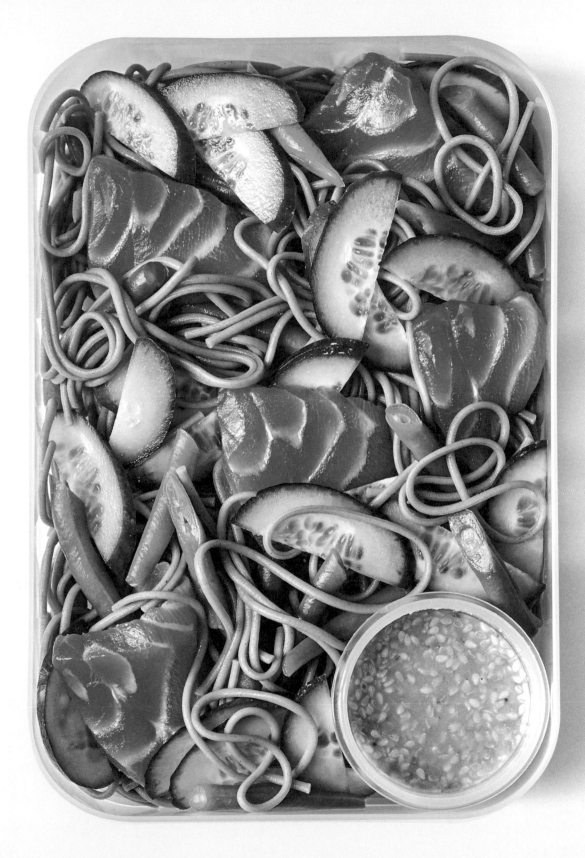

ANTIPASTO NOODLE SALAD

This salad is a simple one to put together – it just requires some shopping at your local Mediterranean or supermarket deli. If you prefer, make your own pesto ahead of time for the freshest tasting noodle salad.

100 g (3½ oz) fresh fettuccine pasta

2 roasted red capsicums (bell peppers), sliced

2 marinated artichoke hearts, quartered

6 balls of cherry bocconcini cheese

Pesto dressing, store-bought or see recipe on page 126

1 Cook the pasta in a saucepan of boiling salted water for 2–3 minutes, until cooked, then drain and cool.

2 Toss with the remaining salad ingredients with salt and pepper to taste, then tip into your lunchbox.

3 Pour the dressing over the salad just before serving and toss well.

HERBY ZOODLES
WITH PRAWNS

Mint and the preserved lemon dressing are a great combination with the prawns in this recipe. Zucchini can be bought already spiralised in the fresh vegetable section of most supermarkets.

1 zucchini (courgette), spiralised

5–6 large cooked peeled prawns (shrimp)

100 g (3½ oz) drained tinned cannellini beans

handful of mint leaves

Preserved lemon dressing, store-bought or see recipe on page 126

1 Toss the salad ingredients together with salt and pepper to taste, then tip into your lunchbox.

2 Pour the dressing over the salad just before serving and toss well.

CUCUMBER & GREEN APPLE ZOODLES WITH SALMON

Depending on where you live, hot-smoked salmon is often available in various styles in the cooler section of supermarkets. This recipe calls for pepper-crusted salmon, but you can also use the plain version instead.

◇◇◇◇◇◇◇◇◇◇◇

80 g (2¾ oz) hot-smoked pepper salmon, flaked

1 short cucumber, spiralised into wide ribbons

1 small granny smith apple, cored and spiralised

½ baby fennel, thinly shaved, fronds reserved

Creamy lemon & herb dressing, store-bought or see recipe on page 124

1. Toss the salad ingredients together with salt and pepper to taste, then tip into your lunchbox.

2. Pour the dressing over the salad just before serving and toss well.

THAI RED CURRY CHICKEN ZOODLES

Here's a simple salad version of a Thai chicken curry.
If you prefer, opt for rice noodles instead
of the spiralised vegetables.

| 100 g (3½ oz) shredded cooked chicken |
| 1 carrot, spiralised |
| 1 zucchini (courgette), spiralised |
| handful of mixed Asian herbs, such as Thai basil, Vietnamese mint and coriander (cilantro) |
| Thai red curry dressing, store-bought or see recipe on page 127 |

1 Toss the salad ingredients together with salt and pepper to taste, then tip into your lunchbox.

2 Pour the dressing over the salad just before serving and toss well.

ASPARAGUS & ZUCCHINI ZOODLES

This salad is the perfect choice in spring, when asparagus is at its peak. If you come across it, white asparagus – or a combination of white and green asparagus – could be used here.

1 large zucchini (courgette), spiralised into wide ribbons
5–6 asparagus spears, thinly shaved
large handful of rocket (arugula)
30 g (1 oz) shaved pecorino
Green olive dressing, store-bought or see recipe on page 125

1 Toss the salad ingredients together with salt and pepper to taste, then tip into your lunchbox.

2 Pour the dressing over the salad just before serving and toss well.

CHILLI TUNA & STUFFED RED CAPSICUM PAPPARDELLE

Fortunately there are now many varieties of fresh pasta available in supermarkets – which only take a few minutes to cook through. They are the perfect choice for getting pasta salads organised in 5 minutes.

100 g (3½ oz) fresh pappardelle pasta

95 g (3¼ oz) tin tuna in chilli oil, undrained

4 feta-stuffed baby red capsicums (bell peppers), halved (available from delis)

handful of parsley leaves

Red onion & caper dressing, store-bought or see recipe on page 126

1 Cook the pasta in a saucepan of boiling salted water for 2–3 minutes, until cooked, then drain and cool.

2 Toss with the remaining salad ingredients with salt and pepper to taste, then tip into your lunchbox.

3 Pour the dressing over the salad just before serving and toss well.

PUMPKIN ZOODLE & PROSCIUTTO SALAD

If you have a good spiraliser, you can spiralise many different fruits and vegetables, including the pumpkin zoodles used in this recipe. Alternatively, seek out pre-spiralised vegetables for an even quicker salad.

200 g (7 oz) pumpkin (winter squash) zoodles, blanched, refreshed and cooled

3 prosciutto slices, torn

handful of chopped radicchio

40 g (1½ oz) blue cheese, crumbled

Balsamic dijon dressing, store-bought or see recipe on page 124

 Toss the salad ingredients together with salt and pepper to taste, then tip into your lunchbox.

2 Pour the dressing over the salad just before serving and toss well.

CHICKEN & MANGO NOODLE SALAD

An Asian-inspired noodle salad that uses sweet chilli sauce in the dressing, this salad is best enjoyed in summer, when mangoes are at their peak.

100 g (3½ oz) cooked, rinsed and drained vermicelli noodles

100 g (3½ oz) shredded cooked chicken

½ mango, sliced

handful of coriander (cilantro) leaves

Sweet chilli & lime dressing, store-bought or see recipe on page 127

1 Toss the salad ingredients together with salt and pepper to taste, then tip into your lunchbox.

2 Pour the dressing over the salad just before serving and toss well.

CHICKEN, CABBAGE, PEAR & CARROT ZOODLES

Carrots are not only orange! Good greengrocers
will often stock purple and white carrot varieties,
alongside the more common orange ones. Feel free to
substitute whichever variety you like in this recipe.

◇◇◇◇◇◇◇◇◇◇

100 g (3½ oz) shredded cooked chicken

2 white or purple carrots, spiralised

1 nashi pear, spiralised

handful of finely shredded red cabbage

Ginger vinaigrette dressing, store-bought or see recipe on page 124

1. Toss the salad ingredients together with salt and pepper to taste, then tip into your lunchbox.

2. Pour the dressing over the salad just before serving and toss well.

BENTO
BOXES

JAPANESE BENTO

This bento box is best put together using fresh, excellent-quality sashimi-grade salmon. Fishmongers can help you out here – as well as pre-slicing the fish. Seaweed salad is readily available in Japanese supermarkets, delis and even some sushi shops.

◇◇◇◇◇◇◇◇◇◇

100 g (3½ oz) sashimi-grade raw salmon, sliced

150 g (5½ oz/1 cup) cooked and cooled rice

100 g (3½ oz) cooked edamame beans

60 g (2 oz) store-bought seaweed salad

condiments such as soy sauce, pickled ginger and wasabi paste

1 Place all the ingredients in your bento lunchbox and seal.

FRENCH BENTO

〜〜〜

Take a quick trip to Paris with this French-inspired bento box.
Go for a good-quality pâté, as it's really the star of this lunch.

◇◇◇◇◇◇◇◇◇

100 g (3½ oz) chicken liver pâté
60 g (2 oz) brie
4 baguette slices, toasted
small handful of cornichons
handful of grapes

1 Place all the ingredients in your bento lunchbox and seal.

ITALIAN BENTO

Burrata is a cream-filled mozzarella cheese ball. It's addictively delicious and rich – and the perfect accompaniment to the other ingredients in this Italian-inspired bento. If you prefer, however, feel free to replace the burrata with a fresh mozzarella ball instead – it'll be a little less messy!

---

60 g (2 oz) salami

1 burrata

handful of cherry tomatoes, halved

3 tablespoons store-bought basil pesto

handful of taralli rings, grissini or sliced focaccia

1 Place all the ingredients in your bento lunchbox and seal.

GREEK BENTO

~~~~~~

The ingredients in this bento are all easy to find at the deli counter of most supermarkets or specialist Greek (or Italian) stores. If you like, include a lemon wedge for squeezing over before diving in.

◇◇◇◇◇◇◇◇◇◇

4 dolmades

80 g (2¾ oz) pickled octopus

50 g (1¾ oz) marinated feta, cubed

handful of marinated kalamata olives

1 small pita bread, sliced into wedges

1 Place all the ingredients in your bento lunchbox and seal.

DANISH SMØRREBRØD BENTO

Scandinavia beckons with this winning combination of smoked fish, cream cheese and rye bread. Smoked fish can be found in most supermarkets – or in more varieties at specialist delis.

75 g (2½ oz) smoked fish
2 boiled eggs
40 g (1½ oz) cream cheese or crème fraîche
red onion slices
rye bread slices

1 Place all the ingredients in your bento lunchbox and seal.

VEGAN BENTO

This satisfyingly healthy bento delivers on taste and crunchiness. Cashew cheese and avocado dip are available in supermarkets, food markets and specialist retailers, but are easy to make as well, if you prefer.

◇◇◇◇◇◇◇◇◇◇

100 g (3½ oz) vegetable crudités
60 g (2 oz) vegan cashew cheese
4 tablespoons avocado dip
handful of beetroot (beet) or veggie crackers
handful of tamari nuts or goji berry nut trail mix

1 Place all the ingredients in your bento lunchbox and seal.

NY DELI BENTO

Take a trip to New York from the comfort of your lunchtime bento! Pastrami is a classic NY deli meat made from beef. There are different styles and qualities of pastrami available – so shop around and find the most delicious variety you can.

◇◇◇◇◇◇◇◇◇◇

80 g (2¾ oz) sliced pastrami

150 g (5½ oz/½ cup) store-bought potato salad

3 tablespoons beetroot (beet) sauerkraut

2 dill pickles, sliced

pumpernickel bread slices, spread with mustard

1 Place all the ingredients in your bento lunchbox and seal.

ALL-DAY BREAKFAST BENTO

Hard-boiled eggs are a great addition to a bento box – adding flavour and a natural protein boost. If you prefer to save time in the morning when putting your bento together, pre-cook your eggs and store in the fridge for up to a week.

◇◇◇◇◇◇◇◇◇◇

2 hard-boiled eggs

50 g (1¾ oz) double-smoked ham, sliced

1 English muffin, split, toasted and buttered

1 tomato, sliced

½ avocado, sliced

1 Place all the ingredients in your bento lunchbox and seal.

5-INGREDIENT DRESSINGS

Combine the dressing ingredients with salt and pepper to
taste in a small jar or container with a tight-fitting lid.

ALMOND MISO DRESSING

2 tablespoons orange juice
1½ tablespoons almond butter
1 tablespoon rice wine vinegar
2 teaspoons white miso paste
2 teaspoons toasted sesame seeds

BALSAMIC DIJON DRESSING

2 tablespoons extra virgin olive oil
1 tablespoon balsamic vinegar
1 teaspoon dijon mustard
1 teaspoon honey

CORIANDER CAESAR DRESSING

2½ tablespoons mayonnaise
1 tablespoon finely chopped
coriander (cilantro) leaves
1 anchovy fillet, finely chopped
2 teaspoons lime juice
¼ teaspoon minced garlic

CREAMY DILL DRESSING

3 tablespoons Greek yoghurt
juice and zest of ½ lemon
2 teaspoons finely chopped dill
½ teaspoon minced garlic

CREAMY LEMON & HERB DRESSING

3 tablespoons crème fraîche
2 teaspoons lemon juice
2 teaspoons finely chopped dill leaves
2 teaspoons finely chopped mint leaves

GINGER SOY DRESSING

1½ tablespoons macadamia oil or
other mild-flavoured oil
1 tablespoon rice wine vinegar
1 tablespoon tamari or soy sauce
2 teaspoons minced ginger
1 teaspoon toasted sesame oil

GINGER VINAIGRETTE DRESSING

1½ tablespoons rice vinegar
1½ tablespoons mirin
2 teaspoons toasted sesame oil
2 teaspoons toasted sesame seeds
1 teaspoon minced ginger

GREEN GODDESS DRESSING

3 tablespoons Greek yoghurt
1 tablespoon finely chopped herbs,
such as basil, tarragon and chives
1 teaspoon lemon juice
½ teaspoon dijon mustard

GREEN OLIVE DRESSING

4–5 small green olives, finely chopped
1 tablespoon lemon juice
2 teaspoons extra virgin olive oil
1 teaspoon finely chopped parsley leaves

JALAPEÑO YOGHURT DRESSING

2 tablespoons Greek yoghurt
juice of 1 lime
1 tablespoon finely chopped
pickled jalapeños

HARISSA YOGHURT DRESSING

3 tablespoons Greek yoghurt
2 teaspoons lemon juice
1 teaspoon harissa paste
1 teaspoon pomegranate molasses

LEMON & SUMAC DRESSING

2 tablespoons extra virgin olive oil
juice and zest of ½ lemon
1 tablespoon finely diced shallot
2 teaspoons chopped mint leaves
½ teaspoon ground sumac

HERBED CREAM CHEESE

4 tablespoons cream cheese
1 tablespoon finely chopped herbs,
such as chives, dill and parsley
1 teaspoon baby capers
½ teaspoon finely grated lemon zest

LEMON DRESSING

2 tablespoons extra virgin olive oil
juice of ½ lemon

LEMONY TAHINI DRESSING

2 tablespoons tahini
1 tablespoon Greek yoghurt
1 tablespoon lemon juice
½ teaspoon minced garlic

HONEY MUSTARD MAYONNAISE

2½ tablespoons mayonnaise
1 teaspoon dijon mustard
1 teaspoon honey

HORSERADISH MAYONNAISE

2 tablespoons mayonnaise
1 teaspoon minced horseradish
1 teaspoon lemon zest

PARSLEY & CAPER DRESSING

1½ tablespoons extra virgin olive oil
zest and juice of ½ lemon
3 teaspoons chopped parsley leaves
1 teaspoon baby capers

ITALIAN VINAIGRETTE

2 teaspoons extra virgin olive oil
1 teaspoon red wine vinegar
¼ teaspoon dried Italian herb mix

PARSLEY & PAPRIKA DRESSING

1½ tablespoons extra virgin olive oil
1½ tablespoons Spanish sherry vinegar
1 tablespoon chopped parsley leaves
½ teaspoon smoked paprika

PESTO DRESSING

2 tablespoons store-bought pesto
1 tablespoon red wine vinegar
pinch of dried chilli flakes

PESTO MAYO DRESSING

2 tablespoons store-bought pesto
1 tablespoon mayonnaise
2 teaspoons lemon juice

POMEGRANATE DRESSING

1½ tablespoons extra virgin olive oil
1½ tablespoons lemon juice
3 teaspoons diced red onion
2 teaspoons pomegranate molasses
1 teaspoon za'atar spice mix

PRESERVED LEMON & HONEY DRESSING

¼ preserved lemon skin, finely chopped
juice of ½ lemon
1 teaspoon honey
1½ teaspoons dijon mustard
2 tablespoons extra virgin olive oil

PRESERVED LEMON DRESSING

2 tablespoons extra virgin olive oil
1½ tablespoons lemon juice
¼ preserved lemon skin, finely chopped
pinch of dried chilli flakes

RANCH MAYONNAISE

2½ tablespoons mayonnaise
2 teaspoons buttermilk
¼ teaspoon minced garlic
1 teaspoon each chopped dill and chives

RED ONION & CAPER DRESSING

2 tablespoons lemon juice
1½ tablespoons extra virgin olive oil
1½ tablespoons finely chopped red onion
1½ teaspoons baby capers

SESAME & GINGER DRESSING

1 tablespoon rice wine vinegar
1 tablespoon soy sauce or tamari
1 teaspoon minced ginger
½ teaspoon sesame oil

SESAME MISO DRESSING

1 tablespoon white miso paste
1 tablespoon rice wine vinegar
1 tablespoon mirin
2 teaspoons toasted sesame seeds
1 teaspoon minced ginger

SHERRY VINEGAR & MUSTARD DRESSING

2 tablespoons extra virgin olive oil
1½ tablespoons Spanish sherry vinegar
1 teaspoon honey
1 teaspoon wholegrain mustard

SHERRY VINEGAR & SHALLOT DRESSING

2 tablespoons extra virgin olive oil
1½ tablespoons Spanish sherry vinegar
1 tablespoon finely diced shallot
2 teaspoons honey

SOY & WASABI DRESSING

1½ tablespoons soy sauce or tamari
1 tablespoon rice wine vinegar
2 teaspoons toasted sesame oil
1 teaspoon wasabi paste (or to taste)
1 teaspoon honey

SPICY JALAPEÑO DRESSING

1 tablespoon extra virgin olive oil
1 tablespoon lime juice
1 teaspoon green Tabasco or other
green jalapeño sauce

SPICY PEANUT DRESSING

3 tablespoons peanut butter
1½ tablespoons rice wine vinegar
1 teaspoon toasted sesame oil
1 teaspoon sriracha sauce
juice of ½ lime

SWEET CHILLI & LIME DRESSING

2½ tablespoons sweet chilli sauce
juice and zest of ½ lime
2 teaspoons finely chopped red onion
2 teaspoons finely chopped mint leaves
1 teaspoon minced ginger

SWEET CHILLI SOY DRESSING

1½ tablespoons soy sauce or tamari
1½ tablespoons sweet chilli sauce
2 teaspoons rice wine vinegar
1 teaspoon toasted sesame oil
1 spring onion (scallion), thinly sliced

TAHINI SAUCE

1 tablespoon tahini
1 tablespoon lemon juice
½ teaspoon minced baby capers
½ teaspoon dijon mustard

TAHINI YOGHURT SAUCE

2 tablespoons Greek yoghurt
1 teaspoon tahini
1 teaspoon lemon juice
1 teaspoon finely chopped
parsley leaves
½ teaspoon minced garlic

TANDOORI YOGHURT SAUCE

2½ tablespoons Greek yoghurt
1 tablespoon finely chopped mint leaves
1 teaspoon tandoori paste
1 teaspoon lemon juice

THAI RED CURRY DRESSING

2 tablespoons coconut cream
1 teaspoon mirin
1 teaspoon store-bought
Thai red curry paste
juice and zest of ½ lime

WHITE BALSAMIC DRESSING

2 tablespoons extra virgin olive oil
1½ tablespoons white balsamic vinegar
1 teaspoon dijon mustard
1 teaspoon honey

INDEX

Smith Street Books

Published in 2021 by Smith Street Books
Naarm | Melbourne | Australia
smithstreetbooks.com

Hardcover ISBN: 9781925811957
Flexi-bound ISBN: 9781922417282

Publisher: Paul McNally
Editor: Katri Hilden
Design: Kate Barraclough
Layout: Heather Menzies, Studio31 Graphics
Photographer: Chris Middleton
Food stylist: Deborah Kaloper

Printed & bound in China by C&C Offset Printing Co., Ltd.

Book 151
10 9 8 7 6 5 4 3 2 1